SHINE THE SPOTLIGHT ON YOU!

A step-by-step guide to building & amplifying your personal brand

LISA GIBSON

ISBN: 978-1-0689887-0-7

www.ignitecommunications.ca
The advice and strategies found within may not be suitable for every situation. This work is sold with the understanding that neither the author nor the publisher is held responsible for the results accrued from the advice in this book.

DEDICATION

This book is dedicated to James, Austin and Molly. You have enriched my life in countless ways and I am deeply grateful to each of you.

TABLE OF CONTENTS

INTRODUCTION

Hi there!

I'm guessing if you're reading this book, you want to move from being just another face in the crowd to someone who stands out, but you aren't sure how to harness your unique experience, values, and passions and present them to the world.

Welcome to the book that's about to become your personal branding bible. Whether you're early in your career, a seasoned professional, or a C-suite leader, this book is for you! Because let's face it, if your brand isn't standing out in this digital age, it's blending in.

Now, you might be thinking, "But I am not an influencer, YouTube creator, or celebrity, so why do I need a personal brand?" Great question and exactly why you need this book, which explains what a personal brand can do for you, helps you define your unique value and tackle potential barriers, and teaches you how to build a personal brand that shines.

When building a personal brand, many struggle with knowing where to start and lacking the confidence to dive in. You may feel overwhelmed by the process, or if you have imposter syndrome, you might ask, "Why would anyone want to hear from me?"

That's where I come in! I have more than 30 years of experience in personal brand development and have helped early-in-career professionals and C-suite executives from some of the world's top companies. I am also a professional speaker on the subject and have a deep passion for helping people successfully build and amplify their brands. Over the years, people have suggested I write a book to share what I have learned about building, amplifying, and evolving personal brands. So here we are. I have taken three decades of experience, learning, and insight and distilled them into both actionable advice you can start applying today and a step-by-step process that will take you from being a hidden gem to a standout brand.

Throughout the book I share personal stories, insights, tips, and practical exercises to help you discover and amplify your unique value and brand essence. From defining your target audience to creating compelling content that engages that target audience, this book has it covered.

By applying the advice in this book, you'll create a personal brand that brings you pride and helps you stand out and achieve the success you deserve. Let's dive in!

PART I
LAYING THE FOUNDATION

Before you take the time to build your personal brand, you need to have clarity on what a brand is (and what it isn't) and what it can do for you.

Additionally, it's crucial to address and overcome personal doubts, such as imposter syndrome, so you can confidently lay the foundation for a strong and authentic personal brand.

CHAPTER ONE

THE POWER OF A PERSONAL BRAND AND WHY IT MATTERS

"Your brand is what other people say about you when you're not in the room."
—*Jeff Bezos, founder of Amazon*

During a recent vacation I was thinking about the evolution of personal branding. Depending on your age, you may find it difficult to imagine working in a world without email, laptops, and LinkedIn. But if you're closer to my age, you may flash back to days of using Wite-Out and the fax machine. This was my reality when I started working more than 30 years ago. I can still remember when I set up my first email account, accessed the internet for the first time at work, and was issued my first laptop.

Fast-forward to today where technology is evolving at an incredible pace. Generative AI is exploding with new products, services, and features every day. Social media platforms continue to appear, evolve, or fade into the background. (I still can't get used to saying X instead of Twitter.) When it comes to personal branding, technology is a double-edged sword. On the one hand, social media provides unprecedented reach—with a single post you can connect with a global audience, and your message crosses borders, time zones, and demographics. On the other hand, the sheer volume of content can drown your voice.

Our data is constantly collected, and like it or not, our personal information is more public than ever before. I am not sharing this to scare you, but to underscore a point: Executives and aspiring leaders need to be conscious of both their online and offline reputation. And to build an authentic personal brand, both need to align. That's why standing out requires a strategic approach, consistent engagement, and authentic interactions. It's also why the impression you make is as crucial as your skillset.

What is personal branding?

Personal branding is the ongoing process of establishing a prescribed image or impression in the mind of others about an individual.

I like this definition of personal branding for several reasons: it focuses on it being an ongoing process and highlights the main point, leaving an impression.

It's ongoing

Let's start with the reference to branding being *ongoing*. Building an effective brand profile isn't a one-and-done task. Think about the thought leaders in your industry. Now do a quick Google search. Their speaking opportunities, posts, articles, and media interviews will populate the screen with corresponding dates. If their activities are dated several months or years ago, what is your perception? Typically, I think "outdated" or even wonder if they have left the field completely. Continuing to amplify your brand profile reinforces that you are not only still credible, but also relevant. Branding is an ongoing process of being aware of industry trends, understanding current issues or challenges, and sharing timely and relevant insights.

Another reason I like the reference to the ongoing process is because it allows for brand evolution. I am a great example of brand evolution. Part of my current brand centers around AI: I am deeply passionate about the power of AI for communicators, and I often post content, speak at conferences, and coach communicators on how to use AI in their daily work. That wasn't always the case because AI didn't even exist when I started working. My goals have also changed. I achieved my original goal of wanting to be a people leader at an organization and then became the founder of my own consulting company. Goals change, perspectives change, and so too, may your audience and brand narrative.

It's a process

I admit the word *process* often gives me hives. However, defining personal branding as a process resonates with me because building a personal brand takes deliberate and intentional action in the form of a step-by-step process. We will explore that process shortly, but at this stage I should mention that the ongoing process of building a brand takes time. How much time you devote is up to you and what you want to achieve. The good news is that in chapters ten and eleven, you can implement proven tips and tools to help you maximize your time and delegate some of the process.

It leaves an impression

I also like the reference to leaving behind an impression. Per Jeff Bezos, your personal brand is what people say about you when you leave the room. When people hear your name, what ideas come to mind? A personal brand strategy helps connect your name with what you want to be known for. A personal brand should reflect who you are: what you stand for, believe in, and what value you offer. But if creating a personal brand takes time and is an ongoing process, why bother?

Why does having a personal brand matter?

Everyone has competing priorities and things they must focus on daily, so why invest the time, energy, and money into building a brand? Because if done correctly, a personal brand can impact buyers' decisions, attract key talent, engage employees, and help advance your career.

Impacting buyers' decisions

> *Traditional company branding and digital marketing efforts are no longer sufficient. Especially in B2B environments, executive branding is now considered a necessity.*
>
> *—Steve Olenski and Kent Huffman*

Over the last five years, digital transformation accelerated all over the globe. Organizations and individuals are integrating digital technology into all areas of life, fundamentally changing how they operate, communicate, and deliver value. As organizations turned to remote work, employees increased their amount of online time, including time spent scrolling social media. A recent survey found that 56 percent of professionals stated that a business executive's presence on social media positively influences their purchase decision, and 66 percent of professionals said they would be more likely to recommend a company or brand if they followed a company executive on social media.

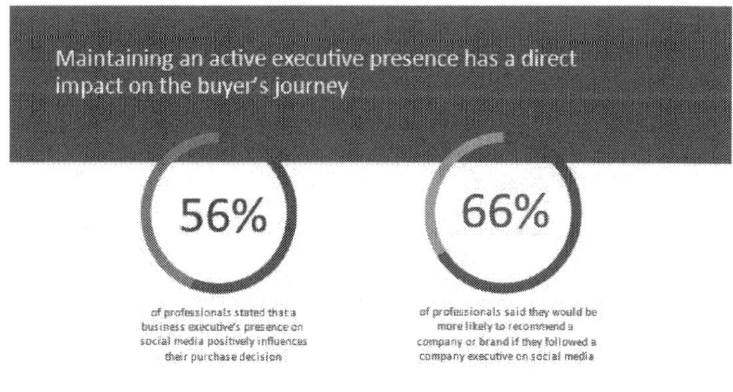

Figure 1 The Changing Face of Executive Reputation, 5th ed. (New York: Qnary, 2021), https://www.qnary.com/the-changing-face-of-executive-reputation-2021/.

I am not sharing this statistic to tell you to sell your organization's products on LinkedIn. In fact, later in the book I will explain why you should not do that. However, multiple studies have found that people who trust the leaders of an organization are more likely to purchase products or services from that organization.

For instance, consider the tech CEO who regularly shares insights into industry trends, personal anecdotes, and the company's innovative or sustainable practices. This approach not only humanizes the brand but also fosters trust and transparency, key factors that resonate with today's consumers.

Similarly, when a fashion brand executive uses Instagram to highlight behind-the-scprenes content, including the design process and ethical sourcing, it creates a narrative that appeals to socially conscious consumers. This type of engagement can translate into a loyal customer base that values transparency and authenticity, often leading to word-of-mouth recommendations that are more effective than any advertisement.

These examples illustrate how business executives' strategic use of social media can significantly influence consumer behavior, turning followers into customers and customers into brand ambassadors. But it's not just about sales. A personal brand can also help attract and retain key talent in the organization.

Attracting key talent

In 2016, I received a call from a recruiter about an "exciting senior position with one of the world's leading companies." The company was Microsoft. I had spent over 20 years working in retail and financial services, and I didn't know a lot about Microsoft beyond Word and Windows. Before I returned the headhunter's call, I did what I always do when contemplating a career move: I researched the company online to learn more.

The company culture, opportunity for advancement, and how an organization contributes to broader society have always been important to me, perhaps as much as or more so than salary. I researched Microsoft, its CEO, Satya Nadella, and the leader I would be reporting to directly if I accepted the job. I reviewed Microsoft's social media feeds to see what it stood for, read what media and influencers had to say about it, and, most importantly, studied how employees felt about working for the person I would report to, and the company.

Not only can great personal branding for your company improve the quality of your hires and reduce turnover rates but it can also save you from advertising on expensive recruiters.

—The Human Capital Hub

Without a clear brand and culture, Microsoft wouldn't have attracted key talent. In a competitive job market, an authentic and well-crafted personal brand resonates with potential employees and attracts the *right* employees. For example, when a company's leadership is known for innovation and thought leadership, it naturally attracts individuals who want to work in a forward-thinking environment. Likewise, a leader known for hiring and developing women will attract more women. This alignment of personal and corporate branding can significantly improve the quality of applicants, ensuring that the company attracts individuals who are not only talented but are also a good fit for its culture.

One McKinsey survey found that almost one-third of senior leaders cite finding talent as their most significant managerial challenge.[1] And let's face it, it's expensive to hire external recruiters. A personal brand that attracts talent helps reduce reliance on external recruiters and can lead to substantial cost savings. Companies with a strong employer brand are

---

[1]   Scott Keller, "Attracting and Retaining the Right Talent," McKinsey & Company, November 24, 2017, https://www.mckinsey.com/capabilities/people-and-organizational-performance/our-insights/attracting-and-retaining-the-right-talent.

reported to see up to a 43 percent decrease in cost per hire.[2] By investing in personal branding, companies can build a talent pipeline that is both high-quality and cost-effective.

Engaging employees and retaining talent

When I first started partnering with leaders to help them build their personal brands, the main goal was to help them reach external audiences to increase brand love, attract new fans, and ultimately increase sales. Measuring social media post engagement was one way I evaluated if I was meeting our shared objectives. An executive and I created a LinkedIn post designed to reinforce the company's leadership in diversity and inclusion. The post went up and we started to see the *likes*, *comments*, and *shares* increase. Since I had just started working with this leader, I was thrilled. However, the positive engagement came from a large number of internal employees. Initially, I was a bit disappointed that the engagement wasn't from external audiences. But in a regularly scheduled employee pulse survey a month after the LinkedIn post, employees specifically referenced the leader's profile on LinkedIn and Twitter and said that knowing what the leader stood for was important to them, made them proud to work at the company, and reinforced their desire to stay.

Furthermore, employees shared that they felt encouraged to share the leader's content on their own channels. Why is that

---

[2]   HR Exchange Network Editorial Team, Mason Stevenson, and John Whitaker, "Statistically Proven Employer Branding Success," HR Exchange Network, August 10, 2018, https://www.hrexchangenetwork. com/hr-talent-management/articles/statistically-proven-employer-branding-success.

important? An article from Entrepreneur.com shared these compelling statistics:[3]

- When brand messages are shared by employees on social media, they get 561 percent more reach than the same messages shared by the brand's social media channels.

- Brand messages are reshared 24 times more frequently when posted by an employee versus the brand's social media channels.

- On average, employees have 10 times more followers than their company's social media accounts.

- Content shared by employees receives 8 times more engagement than content shared by brand channels.

- When employees share their leaders' visions and values through their own personal brands, it extends the reach and impact, creating a ripple effect that enhances overall employee engagement.

- Employee turnover can have a significant financial impact on an organization. I once read that the cost of replacing an employee is almost two times the salary of that employee because of recruitment, training, and onboarding. Eek! And that doesn't speak to the cost of employee morale when a team member loses their favorite colleague or must pick up the slack. Leaders must not only attract top talent, but also keep them.

---

[3]   Ryan Erskine, "22 Statistics That Prove the Value of Personal Branding," Entrepreneur, September 13, 2016, https://www.entrepreneur.com/starting-a-business/22-statistics-that-prove-the-value-of-personal-branding/280371.

- Employees today are looking for more than just a paycheck; they want to be part of a story, a mission, and a community. When they identify with the personal brand of their leaders, they feel connected to the company's vision and values. This connection can lead to increased loyalty and lower turnover rates, as employees are more likely to stay with a company that they feel proud to be associated with.

Advancing career goals

It's no surprise that a strong brand presence and connections on LinkedIn can help you land a new job. In fact, a recent survey by Jobvite recently found that 77 percent of recruiters use LinkedIn to reach out to potential candidates.[4] Over the course of my career, I have been lucky enough to have headhunters and in-house recruiters reach out to me about potential job opportunities. Out of curiosity, I've asked some recruiters why they reached out to me. Their answer was my online profile and how it aligned with the position and culture of the organization they were recruiting for. And while it is true that hiring is often based on who you know, several opportunities have come my way through people on LinkedIn I have never met before.

You may be thinking, "Why would I invest time to focus on building a profile if I'm not currently looking for a new job?" Two reasons: First, you may not actually have a choice. Ouch! I know, but it's true. I speak from experience, as it has

---

4   Aleksandar Dimovski, "24 Impressive LinkedIn Recruiting Statistics," GoRemotely (blog), January 10, 2022, https://goremotely.net/blog/linkedin-recruiting-statistics.

happened to me. Restructuring happens—one day you have a job; the next you don't! Second, a strong personal brand doesn't just help you get a job, it can help you advance in your current job. A strong presence internally and externally can influence how your manager, human resources, and other employees view you as a leader. By consistently showcasing your brand, you create multiple impressions that make you memorable and help you stand out in your field and organization.

Knowing the benefits begs the question why doesn't everyone invest in their personal brand? For some, the perceived amount of time to do it right is a barrier. But for the majority of people, it's because they worry about what others will think. They have imposter syndrome. So, let's tackle and overcome that right now so you can shine the spotlight on you and all your amazingness.

CHAPTER TWO

IMPOSTER SYNDROME

In a nutshell, imposter syndrome is the feeling that you aren't good enough, that you don't belong, or in the case of building your personal brand, that you don't have anything to say that anyone will care about. Imposter syndrome makes you doubt yourself, your abilities, and your value. It can affect anyone at any career stage or in any industry. Numerous studies, including research from NerdWallet, found that 78 percent of business leaders experience workplace imposter syndrome. And that number significantly increases when it comes to female leaders.[5]

As I mentioned, about eight years ago, I was approached about a position at Microsoft. It was a dual role: chief of staff and communications. And I almost didn't pursue it despite having more than two decades of experience working in communications. Why? Because I didn't think I was worthy. I remember meeting with the then-president of Microsoft Canada—an incredible female leader who was

---

[5]   Lucy Buchholz, "78% of Business Leaders Experience Imposter Syndrome," March8, December 21, 2022, https://march8.com/articles/78-of-business-leaders-experience-imposter-syndrome.

smart, successful, and inspiring. The entire time we chatted I was thinking, "Why would she ever want to hire me? I have no background in technology." I remember saying to her, "You know I don't have a background in technology, right?" And I can't recall her exact words, but I do remember her saying that she was looking for someone with expertise in communications and leadership regardless of industry. I spent the next several days doubting myself and my experience, but luckily both my mentor and executive coach challenged me on my self-doubt. I was inspired by this woman and Microsoft, I wanted to work with her, and history had shown that I could do the job.

I was offered and accepted the position. Then I attended my first leadership team meeting. I was surrounded by people who had worked for the company for years and, in some cases, decades. These people led teams that brought in millions of dollars in sales. Technically, I was costing the company money because although public relations and marketing provide incredible benefits and help drive sales, businesses consider them a cost. Also, I had no technology background, barely knew what the cloud was, and felt like a total fraud. At the start of every meeting, each person shared the issues, trends, and topics impacting their teams. In that first meeting, I felt sick as it got closer to my turn to share. I *always* had an opinion, but I was suffering from a massive case of imposter syndrome, and I felt like I didn't belong and had nothing of value to contribute.

But here's the thing: Everyone has a story, and everyone's life is interesting to someone.

How do you overcome imposter syndrome?

Over the years, I have received some great tips from mentors and leaders on how they tackled their own imposter syndrome:

Challenge your negative thoughts: One leader shared her struggle with negative thoughts. As she explored them more, she realized they were often fueled by irrational and unrealistic beliefs about herself. So, what did she do? When she had these thoughts, she started asking, "Is this true? Is this based on facts or feelings?" Then, replaced them with more positive and correct thoughts.

Focus on your strengths and achievements: Often we focus on our weaknesses, mistakes, or perceived gaps. Instead, make a list of your skills, unique talents, and achievements. When you start to feel imposter syndrome creep in, review this list.

Focus on insights: If a social media post doesn't get strong engagement, rather than internalize it as failure and beat yourself up, look at it as an opportunity to learn. Was the post too long? Posted at an inopportune time? Remember, sometimes the posts that receive small *likes* actually lead to one impactful email, engagement, or opportunity. Make all perceived failures a learning opportunity.

Write for yourself and your brand, not for others: My partner is incredibly supportive and encouraging. Most times, he's my biggest cheerleader. However, one day I was sitting in the kitchen drafting a post for LinkedIn. He walked by, leaned over my shoulder, read the post, and said, "Um, are you actually going to post that? Will people care?" He thought he was being helpful by providing honest feedback. Even though we work in completely different industries, I decided to listen to him, and I didn't post it. But I kept thinking about it and had a gut feeling that the tips I shared in the post would matter to someone. By the end of the day, I decided to post it despite my partner's comments, thinking, "At most it reaches someone; at worst it doesn't get any engagement, and I learn from it." And, you know what? That post was among my most engaged-with posts. Remember: You know your audience and the value you provide. Sometimes you need to experiment. Post something new or different, see how it performs, and adapt accordingly.

Personal branding is a powerful way to boost your career, your impact, and your influence. Don't let imposter syndrome stop you from sharing your authentic voice with the world.

Get clear on your why

In the next chapter we will dive into the step-by-step process for building your brand. But, before we do, it's critical that you get clear on your why: Why are you building a personal brand? What is your objective? What specific goals are you trying to achieve? This is about why **you** want to build a brand, not your friend or colleague or manager, but **you**.

Remember from chapter one that you have lots of reasons for building your brand. You might be looking for a new job or working toward a promotion. Perhaps you are a sales leader and want to influence your customers' buying decisions. Or you may have just started your own business and want to increase your credibility and reinforce why you are the go-to person in your industry. Whatever the reason, and there can be more than one, your personal brand needs to align with what you want to achieve.

Identify your "why" exercise: Grab a sheet of paper or open your laptop and write out your top one to three objectives for building your personal brand. Write your why on a Post-it note and stick it on your laptop or in some place you can easily refer to it.

Identifying your "why" is a powerful tool in overcoming imposter syndrome. Understanding the deeper purpose behind your personal brand serves as a reminder of your unique value and mission. It helps to counteract self-doubt and feelings of inadequacy by reinforcing your commitment to your goals and the positive impact you will make. By focusing on your "why," you can shift your mindset from self-criticism to self-empowerment, allowing you to navigate challenges with confidence and authenticity.

PART II
BUILDING YOUR BRAND

Now you know what personal branding is, what it isn't, what it can do for you, and how to combat any imposter syndrome that might creep up during brand creation, it's time to build your brand. The biggest mistake people make when they start building a brand is to dive in without any planning. Don't do that. Plan first, using this step-by-step process I have used with people at all stages in their career to successfully build a personal brand.

But before we dive in, a quick story! I worked with a leader of a large global company to build his personal brand, internally and externally. This leader, we will call him Bob, was being groomed for a bigger job, larger team, and larger sales quota. The CEO recognized Bob's potential but felt that to be successful, Bob needed to raise his profile, both internally and externally.

Bob was all in. He understood the value of a personal brand and was very keen to get started. So much so that he started posting social content on a variety of channels, sought out keynotes on a variety of topics, and signed up to lead several internal working groups. His enthusiasm was amazing, but it wasn't planned or targeted.

What happened? Bob was posting, speaking, and volunteering everywhere. But he hadn't given much thought to which audience he should invest his time in, and his content and messaging lacked consistency. In a nutshell, it wasn't clear what he stood for, what his expertise was, and what he wanted to achieve. More importantly, Bob was exhausted.

That's why they called me! Thankfully for Bob, the CEO recognized that while Bob was enthusiastic and committed, he needed to approach personal branding more strategically if it was going to have the desired impact.

> **Key takeaway: Fuel your brand with strategy, not just steam. Because without a map, even enthusiasm can lead you off track.**

If you think that being strategic takes time and feels overwhelming, then keep reading. My step-by-step guide takes some time and planning, but the small investment of time at the outset will have a much greater impact than just winging it. Here we go!

CHAPTER THREE

STEP ONE: DISCOVER YOUR UNIQUE VALUE

Several years into my career, I was working at one of the top retailers in Canada and, by all accounts, was doing well. I was developing and implementing creative public relations (PR) campaigns, acting as a spokesperson, and sharing tips and advice with morning shows and top media outlets. While I loved my job, I really wanted to lead a team. I started watching how managers close to me were leading their teams. Focusing on the managers who got the most recognition and had the most credibility, I thought about what made them so credible. Learning from others, role modeling, etc. is great; however, I made the mistake of thinking that their personal brand—who they were and what they were known for—needed to become my personal brand if I was going to become a manager and respected leader.

Why was this a mistake? Because it wasn't authentic to me. All my life, I have been known as a straight shooter, someone who is direct and honest. As I tried to emulate these managers and take on their personal brands in an effort to propel myself forward, I wasn't being true to who I am. And I felt it, every single day. This was the first time I started thinking about how someone, even someone like me who was early in my career, builds a personal brand and why it is so critical that it be authentic. People may see that you aren't being authentic, which will hurt your credibility in the long term. But for me, even more important than how it could affect my credibility was how it made me feel—like a fake!

Importance of the first step

After working with people at all stages of their careers, across various industries, and in different countries to build their personal brand, I have found that the first step of defining your brand essence—who you are and what you want to be known for—is often where most people get stuck. And since it's the first step, some people don't progress beyond this step, but instead just start posting on social media and booking speaking engagements. Remember Bob? Don't wing it; be planful! It *will* take some reflection on your part, but I have tried-and-true ways to make it easier for you.

If imposter syndrome rears its ugly head during this step and you find yourself thinking, "I don't have a lot of experience and nothing to share" or "There are smarter people with more experience in my industry"—stop, go back, and read chapter two on imposter syndrome again. Remember, you're not an imposter, as each of us has our own experiences, values, passions, and skills that shape who we are and our views. That's what makes us unique.

I really want to underscore the importance of being uniquely you and the value you can bring to others. Yes, many people may have the same job title, work in the same industry, or want the same goals as you, but was their career journey the same as yours? How about the learnings or insights you've gained along the way? You have unique experiences and ideas that you can draw from.

Case in point: I had the unique and incredible experience of working with three CEOs at the same company over an eight-year span. Part of my role was supporting them with their executive communications and brand building. They all worked in the same industry, for the same company, and each had a similar number of years of experience. Was the personal brand strategy that we developed together the same for each of them? No. Why? Because they each had their own values, passions, and experiences even though they held the same position at the same company. And not only were their values and experiences different, but so were their tone and style. In fact, one of them was so different that it took a bit for me to adjust how I worked with him to ensure his brand and communications were authentically him. While the first CEO used a more corporate tone, this CEO would jump on tables or come flying in (literally!) to keynote speaking engagements. I couldn't do a rinse and repeat of the previous CEO's strategy, as it wouldn't be authentic and therefore would never have had the same impact.

> *Key takeaway: People may work in the same industry, with the same title, and maybe even the same number of years of experience as you, but they aren't YOU.*

Who are you and what do you want to be known for?

I use two approaches to help people get crisp on who they are and what they want to be known for. For some, taking the time for self-reflection (self-audit) clarifies their ideas, and for others, they need to understand how they are currently perceived and then identify what resonates with them and what they would like to change (external audit).

Self-audit

Building a personal brand is essentially about crafting and communicating a clear, consistent message about who you are, what you stand for, and the unique value you bring to your field or network. Conducting a self-audit will help you with the following tasks:

- Identify your core values.
- Recognize your passions.
- Assess your skills and experiences.

Not sure where to start? Here's one way to approach it:

- On a sheet of paper, make a timeline that maps out key personal and professional milestones—the pivotal moments or decisions that shaped you. Circle the milestones that made you the proudest and which felt most authentic to you. Then, beneath the timeline write why you selected those milestones, incorporating the values, feelings, and memories they conjure.

- On the back, create a table with three columns and headings. Label the first column Skills & Talents and write down all the things you're good at. Capture skills related to your career, both technical and soft skills.
- Label the second column Passions and list the things you like to do—passions and activities you could do for hours without getting bored.
- Label the third column Values—then refer to the exercise on the previous side of the page where you captured your values—the things most important to you.

This is what my table looked like:

Skills & Talents	Passions	Values
Strategic communications	Writing	Honesty
Executive communications	Mentoring early-in-career	Authenticity
PR/media relations	talent	Giving back to the community
Personal brand development	Public speaking	Having a positive outlook
& amplification	Traveling & learning about	Optimism
Building strong, cohesive	different cultures	Reliability
teams	Volunteering on boards	Delivering with excellence
Writing/speechwriting	Elevating women	
AI for communications	Keeping active	

Self-audit exercise: Grab a piece of paper or open your laptop and either complete your own table (Skills & Talents, Passions, and Values) or if creating tables isn't your thing, reflect on and capture the answers to these questions:

- What are my passions, the things that excite me?
- What are my strengths? Focus on the ones that you are most proud of.
- What are my unique experiences?
- What skills have I developed?

- What challenges do people come to me to help them solve?
- What are my aspirations?

As you do this exercise, don't just think about your career, but keep in mind the skills or experiences you've gained outside of your career, such as through volunteer work, travel, or involvement with sporting or community groups. All of these have helped shape who you are and what makes you uniquely you.

External brand audit

Once I had clarified what I wanted to be known for, I wanted to see if there was a disconnect between that and how I was currently perceived. To figure out what my reputation was, I took two different approaches. You can do one or both of these.

Internet search: Use your friends, Google, or Bing (I am a former Microsoftee after all), to search yourself. I know it sounds funny but think about it. Just like you Google or Bing a potential date or a new doctor or coach to see their experience and what they value most, you can learn a lot by searching yourself. Let's face it, in this digital-first world, digital presence is a huge part of brand presence.

When it comes to personal branding, searching yourself to see how others perceive you is like being a fly on the wall at your own reputation party. Auditing your digital brand helps you in two ways. First, it highlights what others think about you. Often a search will include articles or accomplishments you might have forgotten about. Read them proudly; they are proof of your awesomeness! Second, if you see something you don't like or that no longer resonates with you, it is a chance to think about how you can evolve your narrative to better align with your current brand. Don't worry about personal narratives at this stage; we will get into more detail later in the book.

Ask others: A second approach is to ask trusted friends, family, and colleagues about your reputation. Make a list of people in your network who will (a) be most likely to respond and (b) be honest and forthcoming with their thoughts. Send them an email with a few questions such as: "What words would you use to describe me?" and "What would you say are my top five strengths?" Make sure to share why you're asking them so they understand that you want honest answers and aren't merely looking for an ego boost! And don't forget to thank them.

Analysis exercise: To understand the information you gathered from your digital search and friends and colleagues, do the following analysis:

- **Compile and analyze**—Collect all the feedback and look for common themes.
- **Compare with self-audit**—Compare the external feedback with your self-audit results, circling the strengths and words most often shared and adding descriptors that you hadn't thought of, but that resonate with you.
- **Identify gaps**—Write down the words that you listed on your audit that didn't appear in your digital search

or in your network's responses. This gap signals an opportunity to communicate more effectively.

Getting laser focused

Now that you have your list of milestones, skills, and values—things that make you unique and amazing—congratulate yourself! See, you do have your own unique story, perspective, and opportunities to influence those around you. I suspect your friends' responses revealed many similar themes, as well as attributes and strengths you hadn't thought of.

The trick now is to get crisp on what you *most* want to be known for, the attributes that are authentically you **and** that align with your goals. For example, my friends indicated that my strengths are bringing people together, organizing fun and engaging events and experiences, and being an awesome travel partner and a good cook, to name a few. My self-audit showed some overlap with the strengths they shared, and I was happy to see that what I thought of as a strength also showed up in my external audit.

Now, let's say that one of my whys for building a personal brand is to reinforce that I am a highly sought out facilitator and public speaker. I love doing it and am good at it. Therefore, while I may have a long list of strengths, I would focus on the ones that align with this passion, my experience and skills, and my why. For example, bringing people together and creating an engaging and inclusive experience and environment is a strength I want to continue to build and amplify. While I love cooking and appreciate the compliment from my friends, I may not incorporate that specific skill set and passion into my brand essence and associated narrative. Why? Because when it comes to personal branding, focusing on a few key strengths or passions is far more effective than trying to be a jack-of-all-trades.

> *Key takeaway: You can't be all things to all people. Think about your goals and then pick the strengths that matter most to the people who matter most.*

Brand Pillar Exercise: What does this look like in practice?

- Go back to the table you created and add a fourth column titled Personal Brand Pillars.
- Use this column to bring together what you're good at (Skills & Talents), what you love to do (Passions), and what you value (Values) to create your brand pillars: the top three or four things you want to be known for, your unique value proposition, and your brand essence.

My table ended up looking like this:

Skills & Talents	Passions	Values	Brand Pillars
Strategic communications Executive communications PR/media relations Personal brand development & amplification Building strong, cohesive teams Writing/speechwriting AI for communications	Writing Mentoring early-in-career talent Public speaking Traveling & learning about different cultures Volunteering on not-for-profit boards Elevating women Keeping active	Honesty Authenticity Giving back to the community Having a positive outlook Optimism Reliability Delivering with excellence	Strategic communications leadership Empowerment & mentorship of women in communications and STEM Advocate for accessibility and inclusion

CHAPTER FOUR

STEP TWO: IDENTIFY YOUR TARGET AUDIENCE

One of this chapter's key points is that you can't be all things to all people. Instead, you need to be selective as you think about your target audience. Why? Well, you wouldn't chat quantum physics with guests at a party for the squash club, unless of course you're into that, just as you wouldn't attend a leadership summit and spend your keynote talking about how to make a soufflé. Conversations—verbal or written—are about connection, and connection is about relevance.

The same goes for your personal brand. It's not just about broadcasting who you are; it's about resonating with the right people. And that's why you need to determine your target audience. I heard once (and I wish I could remember who said it so I could credit them) that you should think of your target audience as your brand's best friends. They get you; they need what you are offering, and they're ready to listen. Not everyone you meet is your best friend, and likewise, not everyone you meet is your target audience.

The content that is interesting and helpful for one group may not work for another, and if you try to please everyone, you run the risk of not driving impact with anyone. Even worse, your target audience could start ignoring you and turn to someone more relevant.

So then how do you identify your target audience? The process is a mix of introspection and investigation. Think about who benefits most from your expertise. Who shares your values and interests? Who's already listening? Who attends the same events and reads the same materials as you?

If this sounds too time-consuming, you can hire consultants to assist you with this step. Also, know this is an ongoing process. It doesn't have to be perfect, as you will continue to build your target audience, but you just need to start.

Using fellow colleagues

A common mistake when identifying your target audience is either to discount the impact of your fellow colleagues or to rely too much on them. Your colleagues are often your biggest supporters (outside of our family and friends) and may understand your industry or niche better than most. They also have their own networks, which may align nicely with our personal brands. So don't discount them or their engagement with your content and brand. Having said that, you want to expand your network, ensuring that you include the right external audiences as well.

Using social media

Analyzing social media can also be incredibly helpful. You can use social media to your advantage in these five ways:

- **Engage in social listening:** Monitor keywords, hashtags, and conversations relevant to your niche. Then look at who is following and engaging with that content.
- **Analyze your followers**: Who else do they follow? Someone in their network may have shared interests and would benefit from your expertise.
- **Join Groups and Forums:** Platforms like LinkedIn have Groups and Forums. Join the groups related to your brand essence. This is where you'll find engaged communities discussing topics relevant to you and your brand.
- **Content analysis:** We will discuss content later in the book, but a quick exercise is to look at content that is aligned with your brand and is performing well. Who is engaging with the content? These are likely the people who will respond well to your personal brand.
- **Monitor others**: Who are the influencers in your industry or niche? Look at the content that is most closely aligned with your brand and see who's engaging with it. Chances are, they are part of your potential audience too.

While you might think of your target audience as those in the front row clapping the loudest because they love what you're playing, your target audience should also include those you want to learn from. My target audience includes the people I can help the most and who can help me achieve my goals. But it also includes those in my niche or industry I respect and want to learn from. As you will learn later in the book, the number one way to sustain and evolve your brand is to be a continual learner. When you think about your audience, I encourage you to also include those who will update you on industry changes, those who challenge your views, and those who you can learn from.

Target audience exercise:

- Review the two to four personal brand pillars you noted in the previous exercise.
- Map out the target audiences aligned to your brand essence. Remember to include both internal colleagues and external audiences.
- Need help with the external audiences? Go to the social media platform that you are currently most active on and, using the social media tools mentioned earlier start mapping out who your target audiences are.
- Add or connect with those who fit your target audience, but who are not yet part of your network.

CHAPTER FIVE

STEP THREE: CRAFTING YOUR NARRATIVE

An authentic and honest brand narrative is fundamental today; otherwise, you will simply be edited out.
—*Marco Bizzarri*

To recap, you now know your why, you have chosen the three to five things you want to be known for, and you have identified your target audience. The next step is developing your narrative—the key messages and stories unique to you that align with your brand essence. A brand narrative isn't just about words; it's about emotions, values, and the lasting impression you leave. And as Marco Bizzarri notes, it needs to be honest and authentic to you.

So where do you start?

Recently, I attended a talk given by a content leader at LinkedIn. The topic was using LinkedIn to help build your personal brand. It was a fantastic discussion, and my key takeaway was that audiences want to consume content that is at the intersection of you, your industry, and your organization.

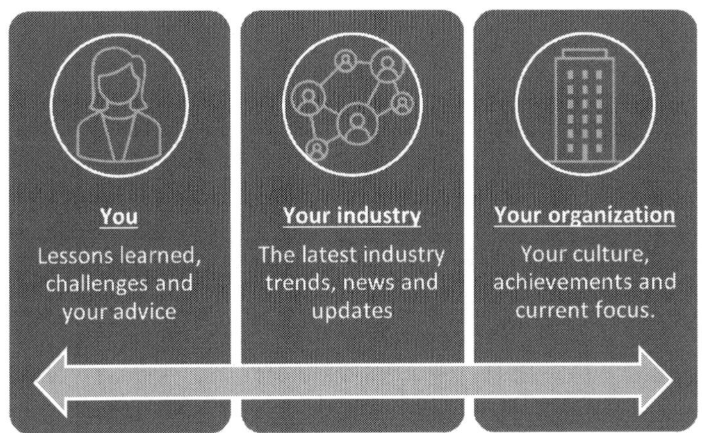

For example, let's say I want to be known for empowering and supporting women in STEM (science, technology, engineering, and math). My narrative might combine my personal experience as a leader in STEM (the *You*), the latest facts and trends relating to women in STEM (*Your industry*), and how my organization has and continues to support women in STEM and drive change (*Your organization*).

Brand narrative exercise

You want to include all three prongs.

The You prong

For many, the toughest part of this three-pronged approach is the *You* prong. The following exercise shows how I approach it when building my own narrative and working with the numerous leaders I support.

In Step One, you built your personal brand pillars. In Step Two, you identified your target audience based on who will benefit most from your experiences and insights. Next, create a new table with three columns that include:

- A column for your three to four personal brand pillars.
- A column to capture your stories and life experiences related to that pillar.
- A column for the lessons learned or insights.

While you fill in the stories and life experiences section, refer to the timeline of milestones you created in chapter four to spark your memory. To demonstrate how this works, let's go back to my example of empowering and supporting women in STEM. Here is what a snippet of my table could look like:

Personal brand pillars	Stories/experiences	Lessons learned/insights
Empowering women in STEM	Share my journey moving from retail industry into technology, including challenges I faced. Stories about how I was often one of the few women in the room at conferences, events, and meetings; how I felt, and what I did to overcome this. Stories about my mentors and how I applied their insights and advice and then translated it to helping other women in STEM.	For each of these stories, identify the key lesson learned and/or a piece of advice that stuck with me and helped me advance or overcome a barrier. How did I apply this to help drive change or mentor another woman in STEM?

Ensure you spend the time to capture all of your stories and experiences. Why? Stories help define your brand as follows:

- Demonstrate your unique experiences and help you stand out from others in your field.
- Reinforce your authenticity.
- Make you seem vulnerable and approachable.
- Build your credibility as someone who has experienced and overcome a particular challenge that your audience might be facing or can relate to.

Industry prong

Once you have completed, the *You* section of the table, continue completing the table by adding industry prong topics for that pillar. For the industry prong of your narrative, add two more columns listing the latest trends and facts, and your perspective.

Topic	Latest trends/facts	My view/perspective
Women in STEM	Latest percent of women in executive positions. Latest percent of women in board positions at tech companies. Most cited barrier for women in STEM. Stats around equity in pay for women in STEM.	My perspective on the numbers and how I envision moving the dial. How I addressed a similar barrier (pull the story and insight from my *you* section above.

Organization prong

Now add the narrative related to your organization: how it is addressing one of the pain points or challenges identified, your role in driving change, and what you think your organization can do to have an even greater impact.

This can be done in one column.

Putting it together

So, in the brand exercise, you have seven columns for one pillar: three for the You prong, three for the Industry prong, and one for the Organization prong.

The next step is to condense these into only three to five key messages for:

- **Clarity**—Your brand should be clear and easy to understand. Too many messages can dilute your brand.
- **Memorability and impact**—Fewer, stronger messages are more likely to be remembered and to have more impact.
- **Consistency**—It's critical that you are consistent with all audiences and across all platforms and in your engagements. Consistency in messaging ensures that your brand's identity is clear and trustworthy, fostering stronger connections and credibility with your audience. A few key messages make being consistent easier and will reinforce your brand essence.

A few other things to keep in mind as you develop your key messages:

- Avoid jargon and overly complex terms.
- Do use plain language that is easily understood.
- Avoid acronyms unless widely known.
- Don't mimic others—your narrative is based on your unique experiences and learnings.
- Do evolve your messaging as you, your organization, and/or your industry evolve.

> **Key takeaway: Do not try to be all things to all people. Three to five authentic key messages will have a greater impact on your audience and your brand.**

Congratulations! You've followed the steps and taken a strategic and thoughtful approach to building your personal brand.

Now that you have laid your brand's foundation, it's time to turn up the volume. Let's shift gears from building to amplifying your brand.

PART III

AMPLIFYING YOUR BRAND

The three Cs of brand amplification: Channels, Content, and Cadence

Remember our friend Bob? The leader who posted on social media and accepted keynotes without a plan or consistent messaging. Well, he's not alone. I have seen many leaders try to amplify their brand before thinking through the channels, content, and cadence that make sense for them and their target audience. This creates confusion about who you are and what you stand for and, as a result, impacts your ability to leverage your brand to achieve your why.

Because the three Cs are the foundation of amplification, in this section, we will explore these ideas:

- The channels you can leverage to amplify your brand.
- How to craft compelling content; and
- What you should consider when determining the cadence of your engagements and content sharing.

Taking the time to create a strategic approach to amplifying your brand will leave you with an actionable plan—one that will engage your audience, be realistic for you and your life, and drive impact. Let's get started!

CHAPTER SIX

STEP FOUR: CHOOSING YOUR CHANNEL(S)

The medium is the message.
—Marshall McLuhan

Marshall McLuhan's now-famous quote means that when it comes to amplifying your personal brand, the medium (channel) you choose to communicate your brand's values and messages is just as important, if not more so, than the content itself. Your choice of channel that you use to communicate with your target audience becomes part of the brand's message, sharpening the audience's perception and engagement with your brand. I use social media, podcasts, speaking opportunities, media (online, print, and broadcast), industry associations, and board memberships.

Clients often ask me if it's critical to use all available channels to amplify a personal brand. While I have seen some leaders successfully use all channels, for others, using many channels is overwhelming, unrealistic, and unnecessary. So, how do you decide which channels to use? It involves a mix of self-awareness, audience understanding, and strategic thinking.

Self-awareness means having a deep understanding of your strengths, preferences, and unique values. For example, if you are a great writer, then long-form blogs or articles might be your best bet. If you are a strong speaker, then you might gravitate toward podcasts or speaking opportunities. And if you are passionate about creating content, then you might focus on social media.

Strategic thinking involves analyzing the strengths and weaknesses of each channel, considering factors such as reach, engagement, and alignment with your brand values.

Of course, you can use all the channels available to you. However, being strategic about how and where you market your brand isn't just about recognizing what you are good at; it's also about recognizing what is feasible for you to do consistently. We will discuss creating cadence and building a detailed content and engagement plan in chapter seven, but for now just know that when it comes to building and maintaining a personal brand, consistency is as important as authenticity.

Understanding your audience means knowing where your audience hangs out and what type of content they prefer. LinkedIn or industry events might be perfect for professionals, while Instagram is the go-to for creatives, and local town halls are ideal for colleagues. The key is to understand where your audience is already active and engage them there.

> **Key takeaway: Amplifying your brand isn't about being everywhere; it's about being where it matters and where it will have the greatest impact.**

So, let's take a moment to better understand the most popular channels that leaders use to amplify their personal brands.

Social media

When most people think about building a brand profile, they immediately think of social media. And for good reason! As noted earlier, a recent survey by LinkedIn found that 56 percent of professionals stated that a business executive's presence on social media positively influences their purchase decision and 66 percent of professionals said they would be more likely to recommend a company or brand if they followed a company executive on social media.[6]

Like technology, social media continues to evolve. Understanding the various platforms, the demographic of each platform, and the type of content that performs best is critical when deciding where you want to amplify your brand.

Choosing your social media platform(s)

Selecting the right social media platform is pivotal for amplifying your personal brand. Remember, the best options are the platforms that are authentic to you, where your audience is already active and engaged, and for which you can consistently create content.

---

[6] "Executive Thought Leadership Quick Start Guide," LinkedIn Marketing Solutions, accessed August 2024, https://business.linkedin. com/marketing-solutions/cx/21/03/executive-thought-leadership-quick-start-guide?trk=lms-blog-b2b&src=bl-po.

If it is authentic to you, your voice will resonate there the most, and if your audience is there, your message will align with the audience that values it most. Let's look at a handful of platforms and their user demographics. Keep in mind that platforms and audience demographics continue to evolve, so you should do a quick search to ensure the following information is still relevant.

Facebook: Widely used across demographics, particularly among older users, Facebook is a versatile platform, and its broad user base can help you reach a wide range of people.

Instagram: Popular among younger audiences, Instagram is a visual platform and, therefore, great for brands where images and videos will play a pivotal role such as food, travel, or design.

LinkedIn: For professionals looking to connect and engage with others in their industry and as a tool for B2B marketing, LinkedIn is the go-to platform. Enabling you to share industry trends and insights, LinkedIn is a great platform to help you expand your professional network and establish yourself as an authority in your industry.

TikTok: Ideal for creators and brands looking to engage a younger demographic. TikTok's format of short-form video content is appealing to those who prefer visual, entertaining, and trend-driven content.

Podcasts

Podcasts have significantly increased in popularity and availability. According to priordata.com, over five million podcasts exist globally with more than 75 million episodes available as of 2024. In terms of weekly listeners, 90 million Americans are reported to be weekly podcast listeners.[7] The pros of using podcasts for personal branding include the following attributes:

- **Personal connection:** Podcasts allow you to speak directly to your audience, creating a sense of connection that is harder to achieve through written content.
- **Authority and expertise:** Podcasts provide a channel for sharing industry trends, sharing insights, personal journeys, and more.
- **Content longevity:** Unlike media articles or posts that can fade into the background, podcast episodes continue to attract new listeners over time.
- **Length of engagement:** Typically, a podcast interview is longer than a media interview or video you would post on social, enabling you to share more content.

You have three options when it comes to podcasts: launch your own podcast, secure an interview on another podcaster's show, or do both. Consider these factors when deciding which route to take:

---

[7] Stefan Larson, "Podcast Statistics for 2024 Listener Stats & Growth," Priori Data (blog), February 21, 2024, https://prioridata.com/data/podcast-statistics/.

- Hosting your own podcast requires consistency, strong production quality (sound, editing), sound quality, a solid pipeline of guests, and high-value content. You will also need to market the podcast.
- Participating in a podcast requires you to select podcasts that align with your brand and enable you to be your authentic self.
- While being a podcast guest requires significantly less time and resources, you still need to take the time to properly prepare.

To evaluate whether a podcast is the right fit for you and your brand, use this checklist:

- **Brand alignment:** Ensure the podcast's themes, tone, and audience complement your personal brand and narrative.
- **Audience reach and engagement:** Ask about the target demographic of the podcast and make sure it corresponds with your target audience. Evaluate the podcast's reach, including listener numbers, social media presence, and distribution channels.
- **Reputation of host:** Evaluate the reputation and influence of the podcast host and note any red flags relative to you and your brand.
- **Content quality:** Listen to a few episodes to assess the quality of the podcast and to make sure the content feels right for your brand.
- **PR and marketing opportunities:** Confirm there are plans to market your appearance, including callouts and tags on relevant social channels.

To become a podcast guest, you may need to proactively source and secure opportunities that align with your brand. Research what podcasts your audience is already listening to and engaging with. Ask your network about their go-to podcast, then listen to multiple episodes so you can evaluate the podcast based on the criteria above.

If after listening to a few you think you're a good fit, you can email the host (or producer) of the podcast. Be sure to include brief information about your background, the topic you want to discuss, why it matters to their listeners, and why you are uniquely qualified to speak about the subject. Offer to set up a call to further discuss your topic and background.

After accepting an invitation, be sure to prepare for your interview and amplify your episode on your social channels. If you have an upcoming speaking engagement or media interview, weave in your podcast appearance, including date, time, and topic, with your audience.

Speaking opportunities

If you, like many, hear the words *keynote* or *speaking opportunity* and immediately feel nauseous and want to run for the hills, bear with me and avoid the urge to skip over this section.

The benefits of speaking opportunities are many:

- Provides a platform for you to be seen and heard
- Establishes your credibility and authority in your industry and field

- Attracts a diverse audience, providing you with the opportunity to expand your network
- Makes your brand more relevant, top-of-mind, and relatable
- Provides a great way to demonstrate your brand essence and personality
- Generates content as speeches and key messages from panels can be repurposed into social posts, blogposts, or podcasts

Yet despite the benefits, many shy away from it because they fear public speaking. This fear (also known as glossophobia) is very common. In fact, it's considered the most common phobia and affects approximately 75 percent of people.

Having glossophobia can impact your professional life, leading to missed opportunities to speak up in a meeting, deliver a presentation, or leverage the power of a keynote—all opportunities to demonstrate your value and reinforce your credibility.

Warren Buffet, Berkshire Hathaway chairman and CEO, recently shared that he believes honing communication skills could increase one's worth by 50 percent because "what's really essential is being able to get others to follow your ideas."[8]

According to an interview with Warren Buffet cited in *Getting There: A Book of Mentors*, good communication skills didn't come naturally to Buffett: "Up until the age of 20, I was absolutely unable to speak in public. Just the thought of

---

[8]   Warren Buffett quoted in Gillian Zoe Segal, *Getting There: A Book of Mentors* (New York City: Abrams Image, 2015), 43.

it made me physically ill." Buffet decided to invest in himself by taking a public speaking course. He shared that after he finished the course, he looked for speaking opportunities so that he wouldn't go back to where he started. "As soon as the course was over, I went to the University of Omaha and said, 'I want to start teaching.' I knew that if I did not speak in front of people quickly, I would lapse back to where I'd started. I just kept doing it, and now you can't stop me from talking!"[9]

Taking a course is one way to get over your fear of public speaking. Starting small and building confidence is another way.

I love delivering keynotes, but this wasn't always the case! I used to get sweaty just thinking about speaking up in class or in a meeting, let alone getting on a stage and delivering remarks to a large, live audience. However, a mentor gave me great advice about how to build up my confidence and ultimately, to develop an affinity for public speaking. Her advice was to start with smaller events, rather than jump into a keynote, and to build confidence by participating on a panel or as part of a fireside chat because multiple speakers mean a shared spotlight, and often, less speaking time.

Because of this advice, my speaking journey started with a panel at my organization's internal town hall. Knowing that other colleagues were participating, and that we would divide the time equally, made me feel much more comfortable. So, when asked if I would participate, I said yes. Was I still

---

[9]   Gillian Zoe Segal, *Getting There.*

nervous? Heck, yeah! If I am being honest, I worried about it every day until the big event.

There is nothing like fear to motivate deep preparation. I invested time in drafting my key messages and engaged my partner to help me rehearse multiple times. It turned out to be a fantastic, empowering experience that set the stage (bad pun intended) for a future of delivering keynotes and facilitating offsite meetings.

So don't let fear stand in your way. Seek out speaking opportunities to reinforce your credibility and amplify your brand. But like podcast opportunities, it's critical to select opportunities that are right for your brand. Speaking at events unrelated to your brand or to a mismatched audience is not only a waste of time and effort given the preparation required but it can also dilute your message, pigeon-hole you to certain audiences and topics, and can negatively impact your perceived level of authenticity and reputation.

So before agreeing to a speaking opportunity, do your homework! Use the checklist below to help you evaluate whether a potential speaking opportunity is right for you and your brand:

- **Relevance:** Does the event theme and session topic align with your expertise and key narrative of your personal brand? Can your existing content be easily adapted for the audience?
- **Audience:** Who is attending this event? Is the audience comprised of people who would benefit from your message? Is there an opportunity to expand your target audience?

- **Goal alignment:** Go back to your why and answer this: Will participating in this event help you achieve one or more of your objectives?
- **Organizational alignment:** Are the organization's values and reputation aligned with your personal brand? Will participating in the event help boost your credibility and positively impact your reputation?
- **Speaker lineup:** Who else is speaking at the event? What is their reputation and level of credibility? Do they feel right for your brand?
- **Logistics:** Do you have enough prep time? Does the location, length of your speaking session, and format of the event feel appropriate and aligned with your brand?
- **Amplification and promotional potential:** Is there an opportunity for pre/post content creation and amplification aligned to your personal brand? Is there a networking component that will enable you to connect with other thought leaders, potential clients, or partners?
- **Compensation:** If compensation is one of your goals, does the speaking fee or gift-in-kind feel appropriate for the level of preparation required and perceived benefit to you?

> *Key takeaway: Speaking opportunities, large and small, can have an incredible impact on you and your brand. For maximum impact, focus on quality not quantity, ensuring the event, topic, and audience align with your brand. It's better to decline opportunities that don't align with your brand than to compromise*

> *your message or waste valuable resources. Embrace these opportunities, knowing that your preparation and alignment with your brand values will help you overcome any lingering fears. If need be, start small, building your confidence with each opportunity.*

Media as a conduit

Like speaking opportunities, the thought of doing media interviews can send many people into total panic. However, you can engage with media in many ways, and when you're prepared, it isn't as scary as you might think. Engaging with social media helps with your

- **Credibility:** Being featured in a media outlet lends credibility to your brand, positioning you as a thought leader or expert in your industry.
- **Visibility:** Interviews can reach a wider audience than just your own channels.
- **Key message control:** Interviews allow you to directly share your narrative with the audience to help shape their perception of you and your brand.
- **Content:** Participating in an interview also results in print, online, or broadcast content that you can share with your social media channels.

I have been working with media for more than two decades, and I can tell you through experience that most reporters and journalists are friendly—not the *gotcha* types you might envision. Having said that, make sure media opportunities align with your brand and always prepare for the interview.

Before we get into the best practices for preparing for an interview, let's explore media engagement formats and how you should evaluate these opportunities.

Print interviews: While the lines between traditional print and digital formats have blurred, print interviews appear in traditional newspapers and magazines that have a physical circulation. Print interviews allow more in-depth responses and can be done over the phone, via video call, or in person.

Digital interviews: These interviews include podcasts, webinars, or blogs. They attract a targeted audience so are great for niche or specific topics. They result in shareable content and opportunities for additional engagement.

Broadcast interviews: These interviews happen on radio or TV. They have immediate impact and visual appeal, and they enable the interviewee's personality to come through. However, they are often associated with pressure to perform well and only offer a limited time for answers.

In-studio interviews: These interviews are conducted in a professional studio setting and usually have better production quality. For those new to media interviews, however, this format can be intimidating.

Onsite or remote interviews: Interviews that are conducted onsite at your workplace, event venue, or other appropriate location provide visual context for the interview. However, you also risk physical distractions (people, cars, weather), so it's important to ensure you are comfortable prior to the start of the interview.

Doorstep interviews: This type of interview occurs when a reporter or journalist shows up unexpectedly. My least favorite format, these interviews can often feel intense and unexpected, leaving you little or no time for preparation.

Regardless of the format, whether you are evaluating a media request or are proactively pitching an outlet to secure an interview, this checklist will help you determine if it is the right opportunity for you:

- **Credibility and reputation of the outlet and reporter:** Is the reporter and outlet credible with a reputation for being fair? Is the outlet a trusted source?
- **Brand relevance:** Is the topic relevant to your brand, narrative, values, and goals? Does it provide you with an opportunity to demonstrate your expertise and reinforce your credibility? Does the topic create any red flags that could negatively impact your brand?
- **Audience fit:** Who is the target audience and is it a fit for your brand and goals?
- **Other participants:** Who else is the reporter or journalist speaking to? What is their view on the topic and how does it align with your perspective? Do you want to be associated with them? Does having other contributors help build your credibility?
- **Logistics:** Is this the right time for you? Is the interview format and location convenient for you?
- **Media training and preparation:** Is the timing right for you? Do you have the time to prepare? I highly recommend all spokespeople undergo media training prior to engaging with the media. It is a great way to practice landing your messages.

- **Long-term impact:** Think beyond the immediate impact the interview will have and determine if this opportunity enhances or detracts from your brand in the long term.

> *Key takeaway: Decline the interview if you don't have time to prepare, the topic is outside your level of expertise, or if you are uncomfortable with the format or reputation of the outlet. Media engagements are opportunities, not obligations!*

A final note for consideration. Most organizations have a PR team or a consultant that is responsible for proactively securing appropriate media opportunities and for responding to media to determine if an opportunity is a good fit. They can help you with your preparation, including preparing media briefing books and conducting media training. Your organization may also have policies concerning who can participate in interviews and when it is okay to participate in an interview. So, before you engage with the media, connect with your organization's PR team. If you work at a smaller organization without PR resources, I encourage you to engage the services of a seasoned consultant.

Other channels

We have now discussed the channels—social media, podcasts, speaking opportunities, and media engagements—that most people think of when it comes to amplifying their brand. You want to consider two other channels: industry associations and organization boards.

Industry associations

Industry associations bring together professionals in the same field to share trends and ideas, learn from one another, and develop new skills. In addition to national memberships, many associations also have local chapters. Participation in an industry association is voluntary; however, the associations usually charge a membership fee. In addition to providing an incredible network of professionals in your industry, they also represent you, your organization, and your industry and will speak on your behalf to address issues or advance common causes.

When it comes to amplifying your personal brand, you can receive many benefits from being part of an industry association, including:

- **Network and visibility**: Participating in an industry association allows you to expand your network and connect with professionals and thought leaders in your industry. Associations often host special events and conferences where you can meet people, share insights, and demonstrate your expertise. And an added plus—they often serve wine, coffee, and yummy food!
- **Public speaking**: Association conferences, events, and workshops need more than yummy treats and an audience, they also need great leaders—like you—to speak on a panel or to lead a workshop. Speaking at

an association event was my first foray into speaking to external audiences. As I shared, I started my speaking journey with a panel at an internal town hall. It helped build my confidence and led me to an invitation to speak at an International Association of Business Communicators (IABC) conference for communications professionals. Being surrounded by fellow members and industry colleagues made me feel supported, like they were all rooting for me! And I walked away with an expanded network and some great social content.

- **Thought leadership:** Prefer to write than speak? Most industry associations have newsletters or publications, and they are always looking for topic ideas and guest contributors. Writing an article is a great way to demonstrate your expertise among your industry peers.

- **Media:** The media often calls upon associations to speak on behalf of their membership on key trends and issues impacting the industry. Whether it's through articles or broadcast interviews, there could be an opportunity for you to leverage your voice on behalf of your industry. The association will take care of evaluating the outlet and journalist and will help you get prepared. If done well, it enhances your credibility and expands your reach.

> *Key takeaway: Seek out industry associations that are right for you. Get involved—go from being a member to being an active contributor. Your audience and brand will thank you!*

Boards of directors

Years ago, a former manager referred me to the board of a nonprofit organization that helped children with disabilities. He knew the organization had helped change my niece's life, and as a result, I was deeply passionate about the work it did. He also knew its board was looking to expand its expertise in marketing and communications. I was eager to get involved, and it wasn't until I had been part of the board for some time that I realized the benefits it can have on one's personal brand.

As a member of a board, you provide governance and oversight and make critical decisions that help shape the organization's future. At a high level, actively participating on a board enables you to make new connections and to demonstrate and enhance your skills. Participation also provides you with insight into how different industries and organizations operate.

For those of you who are early in your career, you might think that serving on a board is reserved for seasoned executives or industry veterans. I once thought that too! But let me share from firsthand experience—you have more to offer than you realize.

I vividly remember my first board meeting. I was uncomfortable and slightly sweaty, and I felt like the youngest person in the room. I am pretty sure I *was* the youngest person in the room. I kept asking myself "Why the heck would they want someone with my lack of experience on their board?" But I quickly realized that being younger and early in my career was a strength, not a weakness. If you are early in your career, it will be the same for you. Your fresh perspective, digital savvy, and desire to have impact can breathe new life into board discussions. As you contribute your time and talents, you will find your network expanding, your skills sharpening, and your understanding of different industries and organizations deepening.

> ***Key takeaway: Don't wait until you think you are "experienced enough." Raise your hand and discover the value you can bring to the table and the value a board position can have on your brand and career.***

At the risk of sounding like a broken record, here goes! Like everything else we have discussed, be thoughtful when it comes to selecting a board to serve on. And know that like an employment opportunity, you must apply and interview for board positions. In some cases, there is even an election process.

Serving on a board is a long-term commitment, so it's important that you do your research to make sure the board and organization are a good fit. When choosing a board, consider the following:

- **Understand your value**: You can add value to a board no matter your stage of career. The key is recognizing where your unique skills and experience will have the most value. What board would benefit the most from your unique contributions?
- **Follow your passion**: Being a member of a board requires an investment of time. You will enjoy

working for a board more and be more successful if you genuinely believe in the organization and the work it does.

- **Board culture and dynamics**: The culture of a board is critical. How do you find out if it's right for you? Research current members to get a sense of who they are and what they value. Reach out to current and past members to get their perspective. Volunteer at events prior to joining the board. In the interview stage, engage deeply and think of it as a two-way interview. Yes, you need to showcase your value, but it's also your opportunity to ask questions that will help you decide if the board's culture is right for you.

Personal branding extends beyond having a social presence. Actively participating with an industry association or taking on a board position can open doors to new opportunities and connections and provide you with another avenue to amplify your personal brand.

> *Key takeaway: Amplifying your brand isn't about being everywhere; it's about being where it matters and where it will have the greatest impact. The channels that you selected today are just the starting point. You can add to them as your experience and/or time allows.*

We've covered the various channels you can use to amplify your brand. Before we move on to discussing the second C of amplification, take a moment to complete the following exercise to find the channels that resonate with you.

Choose your channel(s) exercise:

- Take out your journal or open your laptop.
- Review your target audience(s) and write down where your audience is most active and engaged. Where do they get their information and where would they be available and open to engage with you and your content?
- Reflect on the various channels available to you. Identify which channels are feasible given your current life and time commitments, as well as your skills, resources, and interests. Don't forget to consider associations or boards that align with your brand and desired impact.

Now that you have identified the channels you will use to amplify your brand, it's time to start creating compelling content.

CHAPTER SEVEN

STEP FIVE: BUILD YOUR CONTENT STRATEGY

By now, I am sure you've noticed a theme running through this entire book: strategy and planning are key ingredients to success. The same applies to creating content to amplify your brand.

When you read the word content what comes to mind? I am willing to bet it is social media posts. And while we are absolutely going to spend some time discussing social media content, I want to reinforce that there are many different types of content, including those listed below, to name just a few.

Owned media and personal websites: These platforms include websites, blogs, podcasts, and YouTube channels. The benefit of these platforms is that you control the content and can showcase your credibility, expertise, and values.

PR coverage: Whether it's an article, TV clip, or radio interview, an earned (unpaid) piece of content provides you and your brand with third-party credibility and a piece of content you can use across your various brand channels.

Sponsored articles: Unlike PR coverage that stems from doing a media interview, you pay for sponsored articles.

While not as credible as earned (PR) coverage and more expensive, sponsored articles enable you to have full control over the content.

Guest blogging: Writing for other websites or industry publications expands your reach and introduces you to new audiences without having to do the heavy lifting of hosting your own blog.

E-books and whitepapers: For those who like to write and have the time, an e-book or whitepaper enables you to demonstrate your expertise on a particular subject. It also provides you with content you can use on your social channels or share on podcasts or in interviews.

Elevator pitches and walking decks: These are ready-made remarks, slides, and videos on a particular topic that align with your brand.

These examples are just a handful of the types of content you can create and use to amplify your brand. But no matter the content, you need a strategy!

Remember Bob, the leader who believed in the power of personal brands and was so enthusiastic that he started posting without clear goals or a strategy? Winging it didn't achieve his goals, so after we worked together to identify his objectives and what he wanted to be known for, our next step was to develop a content strategy to help him amplify his brand.

A content strategy is a thoughtful plan for creating, managing, and distributing content that is aligned with your goals while also meeting the needs of your target audience.

Why is having a content strategy important?

Purposeful content: A well-defined strategy ensures that every piece of your content serves a purpose. It aligns with your business goals and resonates with your audience.

Audience engagement: It makes it easier to tailor content to your audience's needs or pain points, which leads to greater engagement.

Time management: Being strategic and purposeful allows you to invest your time in the content that matters and to easily repurpose and adapt content for your various channels.

Consistency: A content strategy guarantees a pipeline of content and a consistent brand voice across your various channels and content.

Knowing that content strategy is critical for success, you need to effectively build one.

Content strategy framework exercise:

You can build your framework using a spreadsheet in Excel or a table in Word, or you can download a free template from sites like HubSpot or Notion. Regardless of the format you choose, include columns for each of the following:

- **Goals:** Refer back to your personal branding goals. What do you want to achieve? Are you looking to grow your network? Reinforce yourself as a credible thought leader? Change careers? In this section, list well-defined goals and how you will measure success.

- **Audience analysis:** Earlier you identified your audience's pain points and preferences. In this section add those insights for each target audience so you can craft content that meets their needs.

- **Ideas and key message:** Capturing ideas as they pop into your mind is a great way to keep creativity flowing. Once you have the idea, think about the associated key messages that you want to land, ensuring they are aligned with your brand and resonate with your audience.

- **Distribution Channels:** List the channels you selected in the previous exercise.

- **Content formats:** Match the type of content (e.g., video, infographic, long-form article) with the distribution channel, audience, and desired goal. Your strategy should include a mix of content formats across your channels to drive deeper engagement.

- **Content schedule:** Create a schedule that includes the timing of when you will create the content, as well as when it will go live. We will discuss content cadence shortly, but a calendar will help prevent content droughts.

- **Results and insights:** Capture any analytics or insights on the performance of your content. Your content strategy will continue to evolve and making data-driven decisions on what, where, and when to post will help lead to long-term success.

Your content strategy framework will help you create engaging content that keeps your audience waiting for more. So how do you decide what type of content to choose? Much like selecting your channels, it comes down to your time, expertise, and where you want to engage your audience. And the good news? By taking a strategic approach, you can recycle content across various channels, which helps with managing time, keeping the content pipeline full, and bolstering brand consistency.

I mentioned earlier that I have worked with leaders at all stages of their career across a variety of industries to help them build their brand. In my years of experience, I've found that for many leaders, the thought of consistently creating new and compelling content is the number one reason they don't amplify their brand. They struggle to think of content ideas and think the process takes a large chunk of time—time they don't currently have! If this is you, don't panic; keep reading to learn proven tips and tricks to help you create compelling content on a consistent basis while optimizing your time. Let's dive in!

CHAPTER EIGHT
THE POWER OF A PROFILE

The content contained within your social media profile is the introduction to you and your brand. It's the first piece of content your audience will see, so take a few minutes to ensure it has information that quickly paints a picture of you and your brand.

A former colleague reached out to get help with a challenge he was having when trying to amplify his brand on social media. He had evaluated the platforms relative to his goals and audience and had decided to start with LinkedIn. His challenge? He was spending a lot of time on the platform, but his following and engagement weren't growing; his perceived efforts weren't having the impact he thought the time investment deserved.

I went to LinkedIn and reviewed his profile and activity thread and noticed three things:

- His profile was incomplete and outdated. It lacked details and flavor. Yes, he included his current job and where he graduated from, but beyond that he didn't share any key highlights, skills, or perspectives. His photo was taken at least 10 years prior and truthfully, didn't reflect who he is today.

- I also looked at his audience: who he was following and who was following him. While he had a decent number of followers and connections, he wasn't following any groups, networks, or specific thought leaders in his field.
- Finally, I looked at his activity. It was basically a one-way street. He liked a lot of posts; however, he rarely commented on the posts or shared the posts to his network with a comment. And unfortunately, he posted very little unique content.

When I first joined LinkedIn, it was mainly used as a recruitment tool. But an increasing number of professionals now use LinkedIn as a thought leadership and brand-building platform and that is how you should approach the tone and content of your profile. So as such, your profile acts as a digital business card to showcase your thought leadership, expertise, and brand. Since it's a direct reflection of you and your brand, it needs to be complete and up to date.

I first joined LinkedIn with the intent of getting promoted or finding another role, and I completed my profile accordingly. I distinctly recall agonizing over my profile as there weren't any guides or people sharing the dos and don'ts of building a profile. The result? The tone of my profile was very corporate, and the content was a long list of my experience and accomplishments. There was barely a trace of who I was as a person and my photo was one taken several years earlier. I have since updated my profile numerous times and attended several talks given by LinkedIn experts who shared tips and tricks for completing a profile.

Profile creation tips

- **Profile picture and banner:** Use a clear, high-quality photo. The **photo** should be professional, your face visible, and your expression approachable. And most importantly, use a recent photo! I know that some choose to use a selfie, but I prefer professional shots. A **banner** (also called a cover photo) is the horizontal image that appears at the top of your profile. I love the banner as it enables you to personalize your profile and visually communicate who you are and what you do. If you are struggling to find an image that works, use a tool like Canva to generate ideas and get the correct dimensions.

- **Complete all relevant fields in the profile section:** This includes a compelling headline, summary, and work experience. Your headline should be concise and reflect your unique value, skills, and experience. Don't be afraid to inject some personality into your headline!

- **Incorporate relevant keywords:** Using keywords in your company description will help with search visibility.

- **Highlight campaigns and results:** In the Experience section, don't just include job titles and descriptions, but also include specific initiatives, campaigns, or projects you led or contributed to. Share the results or the impact that your work had.

- **Skills and endorsements:** While quality is more important than quantity, be sure to include a mix of skills, including those relevant to your industry, as well as leadership, technical, or technology skills. Prioritize the order, listing the more important skills first. And finally, don't be shy about asking your colleagues, customers, and partners for an endorsement of your skills.

Thankfully, you can now get lots of tips and advice online, so as you update your profile(s) across various platforms, take a minute to look at the latest guidance and trends. The bottom line: Your profile should be complete, updated, and consistent across platforms.

Profile exercise:

Before moving on, take a few minutes to review and update your social media profile(s).

Profile:

- Have you completed all fields in your profile?
- Do you have a photo? Is it good quality and relatively recent?
- Do your unique experiences, skills, and achievements shine through?
- Does your profile align with your personal brand? Is it consistent across platforms?

Audience:

- Are you following and connected with influencers and thought leaders in your industry? Your peers? Colleagues? People who inspire you?
- Have you joined relevant groups and networks?

Okay, now that you are feeling good about your social profile, let's get to the fun part: creating content.

CHAPTER NINE
CREATE COMPELLING CONTENT

Mel Robbins is one of my favorite people to follow. Robbins is an author, speaker, and host of *The Mel Robbins Podcast*, which I eagerly look forward to when it drops. I'm not alone. At the time of writing, *The Mel Robbins Podcast* is syndicated in more than 194 countries, she has millions of followers online, and her videos go viral daily. Every morning, I grab a London Fog (a yummy Earl Grey tea latte and an indulgence I look forward to), put my earbuds in, and go for a long walk. If a new *The Mel Robbins Podcast*[10] episode is available, you can bet I'm listening to Mel.

For a long time, I didn't realize this was my routine; however, it hit me one day when I was walking along, listening to Mel share her insightful advice. And it got me thinking about why it is that I eagerly await her episodes, why I follow her on Instagram, and why I subscribe to her emails.

For me, Robbins' content is so appealing because it's research-based, it addresses some of the challenges that I face, **and** it's highly personal and authentic. Every episode includes a

---

[10] *The Mel Robbins Podcast*, https://www.melrobbins.com/podcast

personal story and a description of a pain point, followed by relatable, easy-to-understand advice regarding the pain point. She's a great storyteller, and after listening to an episode or two, I felt like I was listening to a friend.

What makes content compelling

Robbins's style exemplifies the guidelines outlined below for developing and delivering your content.

When developing and delivering content:

- **Be authentic**: Authenticity is the cornerstone of an effective personal brand. It helps build trust and credibility and sets you apart from other thought leaders in your field. And let's face it—no one likes a phony!
- **Tell compelling stories**: A compelling story captures attention. Stories often evoke emotion, which influences how someone feels about you and your brand. Consider sharing personal stories to make you relatable and trustworthy and to help you stand out from others in your field.
- **Be relatable:** People crave connection. Sharing content that makes you and your experiences relatable helps create that connection.
- **Address your audience's pain points:** Understand your audience's preferences and pain points and create relevant content that provides insights and advice.
- **Encourage engagement:** Whether it's a social media post or a keynote, keep your audience engaged. Ask

open-ended or thought-provoking questions, and insert polls or surveys into your content.

- **Be consistent**: We will talk about how to build a consistent pipeline of content shortly, but the goal here is to share content consistently to keep your audience engaged and looking for more.
- **Use a mix of content:** Include images, photographs, infographics, and videos that tell a story and align with both the platform you are using and your audience. Pay attention to character limits and video lengths.

When developing and delivering content, don't:

- **Be fake:** Stay true to your personality and brand.
- **Copy your competitors:** Avoid the temptation to copy your competitors. Develop a unique voice that reflects your brand's essence and values.
- **Try to be all things to all people:** Know your objective, audience, and key messages.
- **Have a one-way conversation: Engage with** your audience by responding to comments and feedback.
- **Be preachy or salesy**: No one likes to be talked at or to feel like they are in the middle of a sales pitch.

Remember, authenticity and relevance are key. Be genuine, showcase your expertise, and let your personality shine through your content.

Content generation

One of the top reasons people avoid building and amplifying a personal brand is the overwhelming thought of creating and sharing content on a regular basis; it can feel time-consuming and overwhelming. I get it! Yes, it does take time, and it definitely requires thought, but I have steps, tips, and tools that make creating content not only feasible, but … well … maybe even fun!

First, let's review the key elements of a content strategy:

- **Goals:** What you want to achieve.
- **Audience analysis:** Your audience's needs and preferences.
- **Ideas:** If goals are the why and audience is the who, then ideas are the what. The ideas, insights, or messages you plan to share.
- **Distribution channels:** The platforms where you will share your content and engage your audience.
- **Content formats:** The type of content that works best for your chosen channel.
- **Content schedule:** When and how often you will share.

If you completed the exercises in the previous chapters, then you have identified your goals, your target audience, and the channels you will use to amplify your voice. You should be familiar with various content formats and the dos and don'ts of content creation. So, you are well on your way to having an effective content strategy.

Now, let's focus on how you can come up with compelling and effective content ideas. You all know people on social media who always have something interesting to say and who post great content. If you are like me, you wonder, "Where do they get their ideas and how do they have time to post so frequently?" Well, in some cases they hire people (like me!) to help them build their strategy and content, but others have developed good habits and employ tools and techniques to help them.

Early in my career, I attended an industry association event. During the opening keynote, the woman sitting next to me was typing on her phone. Initially, I thought her rude: "Why come if you aren't going to pay attention?" I am embarrassed to admit this, but I must have given her the stink eye because, after the keynote, she leaned over and said, "Sorry if I seemed rude, but I was capturing the speaker's stats and thoughts the speaker shared in my Notes app." Later, I saw on LinkedIn that she had created a social post that included stats and insights from the speaker. She added her own perspective and a photo from the event; she tagged the event and speaker; and she asked for her audience's opinions. This woman had developed good habits and techniques to create content. And guess what? Her post had a ton of engagement.

> *Key takeaway: Sometimes your content will stem from your original thought; sometimes it will be based on an idea from someone else. That's okay! Give credit and add your own spin or perspective to your unique voice.*

After I saw her post on LinkedIn, I started noting stats and insights I learned at industry events too. I wrote them in a notebook or recorded them on my phone. And I extended this habit beyond just industry events and speaking opportunities.

During my morning walks I listen to podcasts, engage with others, or enjoy the quiet for some of my best thinking. I always have my phone with me, though, so if I hear, see, or experience something that might make interesting content, I write it down. I used to make the mistake of thinking, "Oh, that would be a good post or an interesting take on X. I will write it down when I get home." But then I'd run into someone, and by the time I got home, I had completely forgotten. So, now I take notes on my phone immediately.

Ashlyn Carter, founder of Ashlyn Writes, an organization that helps create copy for small businesses, calls this being a "noticer of life."[11] In a recent interview on another great podcast, Carter explained that the practice of writing down one thing that happens to you each day trains you to start noticing activities, thoughts, and ideas from your daily experiences that can be transformed into a story or anecdote for content.

Storytelling can be compelling, and stories don't have to be long or drawn out. Instead, they can be brief anecdotes. So, whether you're walking your dog, watching a hockey game, or at an industry event, take note (literally!) of what's happening

---

[11]   Jenna Kutcher, "AI Can't Do THIS For Your Copywriting Strategy," *The Goal Digger Podcast,* April 22, 2024, Podcast, 45:59, https://podcasts.apple.com/ca/podcast/the-goal-digger-podcast/id1178704872?i=1000653183581.

around you and of your thoughts or perspectives. There may be a story there, and you are building a library of ideas for your content strategy.

Another great way to generate ideas is to think about the things your colleagues, friends, or peers consistently ask your advice about. This correlates to the unique strengths and expertise you identified in chapter three. What advice resonated with them the most? And what type of content will reach those in your network that need the same help and could benefit from your strengths and expertise?

For example, my friends, family, and colleagues often asked for my advice about building thought leadership to help them get promoted, find a new job, or move to a new industry. After a few conversations, I noted the most common pain points, where they got stuck in the process, and what advice had the most impact. From there, I developed a blog post, which turned into speaking opportunities, and now, this book.

You can also generate content ideas by tapping into the trending topics on your favorite platforms. Content centered on trending topics will help your brand stay current, and you already know that your audience will be interested.

To find out what's popular or trending on LinkedIn:

- Follow hashtags related to your industry or interest.
- Pay attention to LinkedIn News on your homepage. LinkedIn curates news stories that are trending across various industries.

- Join Groups on LinkedIn that are relevant to your field. Groups can be valuable sources for trending discussions and content ideas.

Google offers Google Trends, a free tool that allows you to see what is trending in real-time for many topics.

In addition to these resources, surveys, interviews, social media analytics, and other sources can reveal your audience's interests and how you can help them. The key is to keep an open mind and be curious about your industry and your audience.

Content ideation exercise:

- Download a notetaking or journaling app, such as Notion, open a new page in OneNote, or create a section in your journal and start capturing your stories, anecdotes, and content ideas.
- Group your ideas by theme and select those that align with your brand and audience needs.
- Take out your content strategy template. In the ideas section, title the main themes, and underneath the titles, add the key messages, statistics, facts, quotes, and stories that align with each one.
- Identify the channels where you will share content and then consider the best content type for that channel. For example, if you want to share on LinkedIn, the content could be a long-form post with an image; for Instagram, a video would be suitable; and for a speaking opportunity, a keynote presentation and remarks are ideal.

The key to creating a steady pipeline of compelling content is to do the content ideation exercise regularly. I capture ideas almost daily. And once a month I convert those ideas into a content strategy. You need to figure out what timeline works for you, but the key is to start and to be consistent. I can tell you from experience that it gets easier once you get going and build the habit. You just need to start.

Your timeline for content creation also relates to cadence: how often you should share content and how you can save time and avoid burnout while building your content pipeline.

Content cadence

While it's important that you share content on a consistent basis, it's impossible to determine the exact cadence you should follow to be successful. Your right cadence will balance your goals with what is realistic and feasible for you.

I once read that when it comes to your content calendar, you should start with a *minimum viable calendar*—the minimum you know you can realistically and regularly create and publish. In product development, *a minimum viable product* is the simplest version of a product that includes only the essential features needed to satisfy early customers and provide feedback for future development. The concept, popularized by Eric Ries in his book *The Lean Startup*,[12] emphasizes creating a product with minimal resources to test its viability

---

[12]   Eric Ries, *The Lean Startup: How Today's Entrepreneurs Use Continuous Innovation to Create Radically Successful Businesses* (New York: Crown Currency, 2011).

in the market. This approach helps businesses learn about customer needs and preferences with the least effort and cost.

For personal branding, a *minimal viable calendar* for content cadence is similar. Start with the core features or essentials that meet the basic needs of your branding goals and then expand over time. This is a great way to start, particularly if you are new to content creation, because if you build a schedule with unrealistic expectations, you will get frustrated and give up. How many times have you decided to eat better, start exercising, or read more, and rather than starting with feasible steps and building on your success, you set unrealistic goals and threw in the towel as soon as you missed the first milestone? Create a cadence schedule with goals you **know** you can meet.

Another common mistake is posting for the sake of posting. For some, a goal of daily posts works. However, I often see posts that don't offer a lot of value or are overly repetitive (we will get into strategically reusing content shortly!), and I start tuning out those posts and their creators. Yes, you should post on a regular basis, but select the cadence that is right for your goal, your audience, and your ability to generate worthwhile, compelling content. Setting realistic goals is key.

Key takeaways for content creation:

- Be strategic; build a content strategy!
- Regularly capture ideas, stories, and anecdotes.
- Authenticity is key. Share your personal stories, experiences, and insights.

- Deepen your understanding of your audience's pain points and how your experiences and insights can benefit them.
- Consistently share content but be realistic, and remember: quality is more important than quantity.
- Experiment, learn, and adapt.

CHAPTER TEN

LEVERAGING AI FOR YOUR PERSONAL BRAND

During my 30 years of working in the corporate world, I worked with incredibly smart and creative marketing and communications people. When I started consulting, one of the biggest adjustments was not having these people available to me daily for brainstorming and gut-checking ideas. While I still reach out to many former team members and colleagues to pick their brains, I can't bother them every day. But what I can use daily is generative artificial intelligence (GenAI). It's my own personal collaborator that helps generate ideas, check facts, and draft various forms of content.

If you are new to GenAI and wonder how it can help you produce content, let me explain. At its core, GenAI uses existing data and machine learning to produce content. Its models analyze vast amounts of data, absorbing patterns, styles, and nuances. These models learn to mimic the underlying structures present in the data. GenAI responds to specific instructions—called prompts—and it isn't limited to a certain style or genre, which means the possibilities for content creation are huge. The trick is to figure out which prompts lead to the best outcomes, a topic I will cover shortly.

Before we get into the nitty-gritty of how to use AI for content creation, I need to admit that I'm biased. I worked at Microsoft for eight years, and while I experiment with other apps and operating systems, my go-to is Open AI ChatGPT and Microsoft 365 CoPilot (which is embedded with ChatGPT). As a result, my examples and tips are based on how I use OpenAI and Microsoft products. After you finish reading this section, I encourage you to experiment to determine which apps and operating systems work best for you. OK, enough technical talk! Here's how to leverage the power of generative AI to help with content creation.

How to use GenAI

Idea Generation: GenAI can help fine-tune or expand a rough idea for a blog post or social post. It can share sentiment analysis to tell you what your target audience feels about the topic, and it can pinpoint pain points related to the topic. Remember, we talked about the value of trending topics to help with idea generation? Well, guess what? GenAI can also scan articles, social media, and other online sources to identify trending topics. Whether it's a viral hashtag, breaking news, or a cultural moment, GenAI can help you stay on top of what's trending.

Audience demographics: With the right prompts, GenAI can provide a lot of information about your target audience. What do they like? What are their challenges? What motivates them to take action? This information is particularly useful if you are trying to evaluate or engage a new group or target audience.

Research and compelling evidence: Including statistics, survey findings, or relevant quotes in your content lends credibility to your content, and GenAI can help find them. A word of warning: GenAI can make mistakes, so verify the information is accurate before you include it.

Summarizing books or documents: Do you want to craft a post that shares the top insights from a book or an article, or the top findings from a research paper or survey? Include the link to the whitepaper, book, article, or survey, and ask GenAI to summarize its key takeaways. You can also ask for specific page references if you want to go deeper into a particular finding. Turn those takeaways into content.

Writing: If you don't like writing, GenAI is your friend. Whether it's a press release, blog post, social copy, or poetry, GenAI can help you write a great first draft. Notice I said first draft! As good as your prompts might be, you won't get a perfect version on the first go-round. You need to experiment with your prompts, ask for different versions, and edit the draft to ensure it aligns with your voice and brand.

Media pitch and prep: In chapter six, I emphasized the importance of doing your homework to select the right media outlet and of preparing for media interviews. If you don't have access to a PR department or media consultant, GenAI can help you prepare. Use GenAI to identify top reporters or journalists by topic and to review what they have written or said on the topic. You can even ask it to generate the top 5 to 10 most likely and challenging questions on a particular topic. Once armed with this information, ask GenAI how best to respond to those questions based on your target audience. And you can get this wealth of information in a matter of seconds!

Proofing and editing: Finally, whether it's a social post, blog post, sponsored article, or whitepaper, GenAI can edit and proofread your draft. As with everything with GenAI, it can make mistakes, so be sure to do another round of proofreading.

Generating images: GenAI is not just useful for writing and research; you can also use it for generating images. While I prefer to use photography when it's available, using AI image creators like Canva or Dall-e instead of hiring a graphic designer will save money and production time.

These are just a handful of the ways you can use GenAI to help ideate and draft compelling content, but to get GenAI to work for you, you need to know how to ask, and that is where prompting comes in.

The art of the prompt

A prompt is the query, command, or statement you enter when asking a GenAI model (like ChatGPT) to start a response or action using natural language processing. Basically, the prompt tells the model to search for and generate material that is relevant to what you are asking it to do. You need to provide it with the best possible prompts to get the best possible outcome.

To craft a good prompt, follow these tips:

Be specific and clear: Contrary to what some think, GenAI cannot read your mind—at least not for now. So, your prompts need to be clear and precise. Avoid using jargon, vague statements, or ambiguous phrases. Instead, use simple, straightforward language.

Tell it what to do (and what not to do): Be clear about what you want it to do. Do you want to know the top five to seven tips on a particular topic, provided in bullet form? Do you want it to write a blog post using a certain tone—fun, conversational, professional, assertive—and include a specific call to action? Ask it by using those details in your prompt. If you want it to omit extensive detail or offensive language, tell it so in your prompt. The more direction you provide, the better the outcome and the less editing you will have to do.

Provide context: The biggest mistake I made when I first started using ChatGPT was not providing enough context in my prompt. My prompt would be something like "Draft me a blog post with the top five tips for using generative AI." And then I would be unhappy with the response. When I started including more specific directions and context, I got much better results as the output drafted for the correct audience, was in the right tone and was the desired length. An example of a prompt that I used was "Create a blog post that provides the top five tips for using generative AI in marketing communications, with a focus on improving customer engagement and personalizing content. Include case studies or real-world examples relevant to communication professionals."

When drafting prompts, less is not more! To make the prompt more specific, add in:

- **Persona:** Ask the tool to take on a role (executive, business owner, storyteller, or marketer).
- **Audience:** Share details about the audience (employees, customers, media).
- **Parameters**: Include any limitations on length (number of words, bullet points, or tips) and parameters on style or tone.
- **Additional context**: Include which points should be covered and what specific call to action you desire.

My final tip: Experiment and try again! Because perfect first drafts are a myth, experiment in advance so you aren't stressing and trying things with an imminent deadline looming. And, if you don't get what you want, add more context, give it additional direction, and try again.

Limitations

GenAI does have limitations. In addition to sometimes getting the facts wrong, GenAI inherits biases from the training data. So, you need to evaluate the output to confirm that it's fair and unbiased.

Finally, I always give credit where credit is due, even to GenAI, and I suggest you do the same. While you don't need to cite it for general searches and ideation, you may want to cite it for written content or when you have used it extensively: "The ideas presented in this section were generated using AI tools, which facilitated creative brainstorming and exploration."

And by the way, I used AI to create that statement! The world of AI is rapidly changing and will continue to evolve, so it's best to stay updated on copyright guidelines and relevant citation guidelines and to be transparent about your use.

> *Key takeaway: Generative AI isn't just a tool; it's a creative companion. The power is in the prompts, so experiment with different prompts, adapt it to your voice and brand, and remember to always fact check!*

PART FOUR

SUSTAINING AND EVOLVING YOUR BRAND

Congratulations on creating a solid brand. Now you need to keep it going. Even if you use tools like GenAI, creating content still requires ideas and time. So, you need a strategy for sustaining your brand and a way to measure the impact so you can evolve.

CHAPTER ELEVEN

TIPS TO SUSTAIN YOUR BRAND

Creating content can be exhausting and can lead to burn-out. But you can use tricks and tools to help ease the burden, including reused and recycled content, scheduling tools, and social media managers.

Reuse and recycle

Let's switch gears from creating original content to the multiple ways you can reuse and recycle your amazing, high-performing existing content to save time and drive additional impact.

Cross-posting is posting the same content on different channels. The content is posted as is without adapting it. Pretty simple.

Reposting is just how it sounds: reposting the same content on the same channel. How often you repost the content depends on the content. Generally, you want to space it out so it doesn't feel like you are spamming your audience; however, if the content is holiday- or event-related, then it might make sense to repost more frequently during that specific time frame.

Repurposing is taking existing content and adapting it for other formats or channels. According to research by SEMRush, 42 percent of today's marketers say that adding repurposing to their content strategy yields amazing results.[13] Among other things, it helped them successfully reach more segments of their intended audience.

To get your creative juices flowing, use these repurposing ideas:

- Create a blog post or social post from a keynote presentation.
- Break up a whitepaper into multiple shorter blog posts.
- Repackage research to create infographics for LinkedIn or Instagram.
- Pull quotes from a customer case study or thought leadership piece and post them as images on social media.
- Use content from a blog post for a podcast or media interview.

Repurposing content saves time and enables you to reach audiences on different platforms. However, don't post repurposed content on any channel. Remember that the content format must be appropriate for the channel, and as always, it needs to align with your brand and audience needs.

---

[13] Shannon Hilson, "Content Repurposing: Transforming Old Content into New Opportunities," Rock Content (blog), April 8, 2024, https://rockcontent.com/blog/content-repurposing/.

Scheduling content

Many strategies and tools can help you create compelling content and prevent content burnout. The same is true when it comes to publishing your content. Using a tool like Hootsuite, ContentStudio, Sprout Social or SocialPilot enables you to automate tasks, including scheduling and distributing your content.

You can even create and schedule your posts days or weeks in advance to guarantee a consistent drumbeat of content. These tools can also cross-post to multiple social media channels simultaneously, eliminating the need to post on each individual account. Whether you publish yourself or choose to automate, remember that authentic engagement is critical.

Media managers

I have worked with leaders in various ways to help them with their social strategies. Sometimes, I craft the content and they post it. Other times I develop the posts and then use a tool to schedule them. And some people have given me administrative power and access to their profile so that I can post on their behalf. My preference is the latter because then I can see the analytics and evolve the content accordingly. A word of caution if you go this route: Trust the person you hire to handle your social media posts and stay engaged with your content!

At a very minimum, this means knowing what content your brand is putting out there.

There is nothing worse for your credibility than to not be aware of the content of your posts. A leader I worked with was at a dinner party one weekend and another guest commented on an article he had shared. Typically, he would have reviewed the content before I posted it, but in this case, he hadn't, and it was embarrassing that he didn't know what article or post they were referring to. It was a good lesson for both of us. Hiring help is absolutely okay, and sometimes necessary, but you still need to stay engaged with your posts. Set up a process with any person managing your content that allows visibility into the content to confirm it is in your voice, is aligned to your brand, and tells you what the expected publish dates will be.

Engagement

Regardless of whether you create your content or someone else does, content creation alone will not help you succeed, even if you use a social media manager.

You must engage with your audience.

Don't ghost them!

Social media engagement is a two-way street. Now, this might seem obvious, but in my early days, I was so focused on how many people liked, commented, or shared my content that I didn't pay attention to what the comments and reshares actually said, nor did I engage back. I discovered the hard way that interacting with your audience is key. Someone posted a negative comment regarding my content—a comment that I could have easily and quickly addressed—and I failed to see it and respond to it. Eek! The ensuing conversation not only escalated, but it also looked like I was avoiding the feedback.

Whether a response is positive or negative, don't ghost your audience! Acknowledge compliments, address issues, and respond thoughtfully to comments. It will help deepen engagement and strengthen your relationships. To encourage successful engagement, remember the following tips:

Personal touch: Personalized interactions make followers feel valued, encourages them to continue to engage, and increases brand loyalty.

Acknowledge shares and mentions: Beyond commenting, make sure to thank users who share your content or mention you, as this amplifies your reach and makes them feel valued.

Engagement timing: There are pros and cons regarding when you engage. Immediate responses show you are paying attention, but spreading out engagement keeps the conversation going over a longer period and may lead to more visibility because algorithms tend to favor active discussions.

Address negative feedback constructively: When faced with criticism, respond professionally and constructively. This shows you value feedback and are committed to improvement.

> *Key takeaway: Remember, social media is a two-way street. Active engagement is critical for creating a more dynamic and interactive social media strategy that resonates with your audience, builds meaningful relationships with your followers, and strengthens your personal brand.*

CHAPTER TWELVE
MEASURING FOR IMPACT

"What gets measured gets managed."
—Peter Drucker

Successfully building and amplifying a brand isn't one and done, it is a journey. To grow your brand, you need to measure, adapt, and evolve. Metrics and feedback provide tangible evidence of what's working and what's not. Use them to glean insights to help evolve your brand, **not** to beat yourself up or get defeated if your impact isn't as strong as you would like. The reality is that not every piece of content will exceed your Key Performance Indicators targets. (KPIs are quantifiable metrics used to evaluate the success of your content efforts over time). So, jump in with a learning mindset!

When I started my own consulting business, I knew I wanted to evolve my brand. I didn't need a complete overhaul, but I wanted to make some tweaks. I completed the exercises shared in this book and decided that after I launched my website, I would be intentional about posting on LinkedIn. I had spent so much of my time and energy helping others with their profiles and posts that I hadn't been as consistent with my own. So, I started crafting and sharing content, and every few weeks, I reviewed the metrics. My review focused on reach and engagement, yet the post that resulted in a business opportunity didn't have much engagement. Be aware of the measurements and insights that I will explain to you, but remember that to measure impact, you also need to think beyond just reach and engagement.

Defining success metrics

By measuring and analyzing metrics and feedback, you can make data-driven decisions that will help you refine your personal brand so that it remains dynamic and relevant. There are no hard and fast rules when it comes to measurement. What you measure and how you set your targets depends on your goals and the channels you use to amplify your brand. Having said that, you want to set targets that feel lofty, not ones that you know you can easily achieve. *As Michaelangelo reportedly said, "The greatest danger for most of us is not that our aim is too high and we miss it, but that it is too low, and we reach it."*

Here are the quantitative and qualitative metrics I commonly track and analyze when evaluating and evolving personal brands:

Social media metrics

- **Engagement metrics**: Likes, comments, shares, and the average engagement rate of a post.

- **Reach metrics**: Impressions, reach, and follower growth rate. While I focus on the size of my audience, I would rather have quality audience members over quantity.
- **Conversion metrics**: Click-through rates, and conversion from social media profiles to other platforms or sites.

Beyond social metrics

- **Website analytics:** Page views, bounce rate, and time spent on site.
- **Network growth:** New connections, mentions by influencers, invitations to events and speaking opportunities.
- **Media metrics:** Reach, key message pull through (how well your core messages are reflected in media coverage and other communications channels), reader comments, and article shares.

Qualitative measures

- **Audience engagement and feedback:** Keynote survey, audience engagement during Q&A sections, and social sharing of keynote insights or quotes.
- **Repeat requests or referrals:** For podcasts, media interviews, and speaking opportunities.

Don't panic if you read through this list and thought, "How can I possibly track all of this?" Tools like HubSpot, Hootsuite, Google Analytics, and Sprout Social, to name just a few, can help you track metrics from basic engagement to more complex conversion data. The key is to set targets, then track and analyze your results on a consistent basis.

Going beyond the numbers

To successfully sustain and evolve your brand, you need to turn measurement into action. And to do that, you need to interpret the data. Recently, I worked with an executive to improve his LinkedIn profile and build a consistent pipeline of content. I drafted the content, and he posted it. We connected on a quarterly basis to review and discuss his social metrics. While preparing for the meeting, I noticed that one post had incredibly poor engagement relative to the others. My first thought was that the content wasn't interesting or relevant for his audience. But on deeper inspection, I saw that he had posted it at one o'clock in the morning. For context, the majority of his audience is in the same time zone as him. He confirmed he hadn't had the chance to post at the originally scheduled time, so he posted it when he got home from a dinner party. We recycled the content a few days later at the previously scheduled time, and this time, it received lots of engagement. Clearly, it wasn't the content; it was that he posted it when everyone was asleep.

If you see either a spike or a sharp decline in engagement, there could be a specific reason. That is why recognizing patterns is important. Is your audience more active and engaged at certain times of the day? Do they respond better to videos or to written posts? Do they like educational posts with tips and tricks or promotional posts? Tracking metrics over time allows you to see trends and patterns that indicate the long-term health of your brand.

And don't forget to track qualitative measurement. Reviewing feedback and comments also provides good insight into the type of content your followers value and what format they prefer.

Be a continuous learner

Because successfully building and amplifying a personal brand is a journey, the people who are most effective in sustaining and evolving their brands are those who are committed to ongoing learning. They take a proactive and strategic approach to self-improvement and adaptation. Here are a few ways you can be a continuous learner:

- **Stay curious**: Be on the lookout for new trends and key issues impacting your audience. In chapter nine, we talked about how to use social and online tools to identify trending topics.
- **Set aside time for learning**: Whether it's a new skill, understanding a new market, or mastering a new technology or tool, set a goal and schedule time for learning. For example, I block an hour in my calendar a few times a week (typically early morning before my workday starts) to listen to a podcast, read an article, or complete online coursework. If I don't schedule it, it won't happen!
- **Actively and authentically network:** Engaging with peers, mentors, mentees, and industry leaders can

help you stay updated on emerging trends and best practices in your industry.

- **Solicit feedback:** Ask for feedback from your audience and peers.
- **Experiment:** Don't be afraid to try new things and learn from your successes and failures.
- **Review your performance:** Regularly review your content strategy, analyze the data and insights, and update your content accordingly. When I first started on my own personal branding journey, I completed a personal-brand deep dive every month. Now, I prefer to do it every quarter. Whatever your timeline is, schedule the session and stick to it!

Brand strategy deep dive exercise:

Regularly reviewing your personal brand strategy is critical for long-term success. Determine how often you want to complete a deep dive into your personal brand strategy and performance and then schedule review meetings in your calendar.

During this session, ask yourself:

- Does my personal brand strategy still resonate with me and align with my goals?
- What engagement patterns or trends are emerging? Are there particular topics that perform the best, times of the day or week that yield the most comments, or content formats that lead to strong engagement?
- Has my target audience evolved? Have the demographics and preferences of my audiences shifted?

- Have I leveraged vehicles outside of social media to amplify my brand and if so, how impactful were they?
- What new skills or tools should I prioritize learning?
- What do I want to experiment with?

Sometimes we adapt our brands to align to new career goals or to remain relevant to our network. Whatever the reason, the ongoing process of reviewing, learning, and adapting is key to a successful personal brand strategy.

CONCLUSION

BECOMING UNFORGETTABLE

We have covered <u>a lot</u> of information, and if you made it this far, then you deserve big congratulations. From understanding the power of a personal brand to conquering doubts and imposter syndrome, you have laid the foundation for a brand that is uniquely yours. You've discovered your value, defined your audience, and crafted a narrative that will resonate and help you stand out.

Through the strategies, tips, and stories shared, you've learned how to amplify your voice in a world full of noise. You've chosen your channels, built a content strategy, and understood how to harness the power of AI to elevate your presence. You've set up the systems to save time and measure the impact of your efforts.

As you get set to build, evolve, and amplify your brand, remember this is only the beginning of a continuous evolution—a process of learning, growing, and adapting. Trust me: In a world where blending in is the norm, you have the power to stand out.

ACKNOWLEDGMENT

Writing a book has been a dream of mine for some time, and I am incredibly grateful for the guidance and support I received throughout this process. I would like to express my deepest gratitude to my amazing partner, James Stewart, and my mom, Mary Gibson. Without your encouragement and belief in me, this book would not have been possible.

Special thanks to the leaders who entrusted me with building and amplifying their brand. Our work together provided me with experience, insights, and the inspiration to write this book. To my dear friends Chris Davies and Brenda Chow, thank you for your unwavering support during the launch of my business and writing this book.

I'd also like to recognize and thank Sarah Micak, Cayley Kochel, and Elizabeth Hamilton for reading the initial draft of the book and providing helpful edits and feedback.

A special shout-out to selfpublishing.com for providing a step-by-step process, resources, and coaching, and to the editors of Beacon Point LLC for their tremendous editing skills, both of whom greatly enhanced the quality of this work.

Finally, I would like to thank my family and friends for their support and patience throughout this journey. I am so grateful to have such an amazing group of cheerleaders by my side.

Manufactured by Amazon.ca
Bolton, ON